ACCIDENTAL
UNDERDOSE

W

NEWMAN SPRINGS PUBLISHING
320 Broad Street
Red Bank, NJ 07701

First originally published by Newman Springs Publishing 2021

ISBN 978-1-63692-611-7 (Paperback)
ISBN 978-1-63692-612-4 (Digital)

Printed in the United States of America

Concepts Through Reality

This is not a self-help book. It is not a diatribe about the dangers of Al and his entourage, of which there are legions. It's actually an homage, a thank-you for making my life more interesting and filled with laughter and light and darkness and discovery and evil and angels that I probably never would have witnessed without our frequent conversations. And lived to tell the tale. Therefore, I don't recommend my travails to anyone, because in my mind it was all accidental, and I have been assigned, as an encouragement and a karmic duty, to put up warning signs along the road that I had just traversed. I do this gladly and with great gratitude for still being alive, and if it just saves one person, I hope it might be you. So consider me your own personal signpost.

You might call this a semiautobiography because it seems I have thirty-five more years to go to a hundred, so with any luck, it's not over 'til the fat lady sings, and I don't see anyone in the wings awaiting. While the following vignettes sincerely represent the situations involved in each, the truth is here to the best of my recollection. It's also a semi because half the stuff that happened in the last sixty-five years I don't have the space for here or the inclination to recite at this time. I may get back to you on that, but let's stick to this for now, if you don't mind. Sometimes you wonder exactly how many lives do you have anyway? The actual answer is another question. How many would you like? Your choice is the final retort. It will be in my final report.

You will probably note that there is nobody else in this adventure except Al, me, and you. Oh, there are several other characters who wander in and out during circumstances here and there, but they are also fellow travelers who would like to remain anonymous, for various reasons, as do I. If you know me personally, no doubt you'll know me, but the best-kept confidences are the ones no one else is privy to.

So it is in the spirit of the friends of Bill that everything here will be the truth without consequences, in the tradition of your beloved founder, Bill W. Kudos to you, sir, for making conversations possible between disparate and desperate personalities who find they have something in common. Well, I mean besides the whining about your predicaments (I've been to meetings and was impressed by the how-low-can-you-go one-downmanship that is prevalent). It may be more comfortable in a lighted room with a breeze instead of a cigarette smoke-filled basement or vacant storefront by the way. Just a suggestion, nothing personal.

Yeah, that would be Al, the main man, ready at a moment's notice to knock you unconscious and drag you away to the loony bin or jail or the morgue or, worse yet, a remorse you can't remember what for but it's in the back of your mind forever. Take my advice on that. Just forgive *yourself* for being a consummate asshole and start over and get on with your friggin' life. Before you fell down and couldn't get up you used to have one. What happened there? Al became too much of a force in your own little private world, and you started to boohoo all over yourself and others and reached out to people who were and are in the same circumstances. Well, good for you for finding safe sanctuary, but you know that finding safety in numbers only means that the numbers increase as you travel along your lonely road. The rut is filled with lonely souls, so step outside your box and pretend to help a little bit, and remember why you are here. Start here with your bad self. You must forgive me in advance for taking short shrift with ne'er do wells and recalcitrant behavior because, since I am one of that ilk, I feel free to speak freely. Guess what, I have taken my own advice, and I arrogantly presume to have a little experience regarding some but not all of human behavior. I think my guardian angel forgave me before I did myself because he knows more than I do about where I've been and what I've been up to. Probably more than I care to or can remember. Some of it is here, and I hope you will accept it as it is for what it is worth to you. The truth only hurts for a little while, but you have to tell it so the scars and moments in your life that you regret are no longer bound to your soul forever. I have found that there is some freedom after all in resolving the vagaries of your existence and accepting your own private considerations as reality. Now about Al.

RESERVATIONS S'IL VOUS PLAIT

You know Al, he's been around before God, some say, because only Al could have come up with such a cockamamie story about the creation of the universe. Good Lord, what in the world? Who in heaven could think of something more outrageous than creating a universe in seven days—six because Sundays is relax time—when it took five minutes to create New Jersey. Do the math, it just doesn't add up. I'm thinking Al.

So while looking through old *National Geographic* magazines as a kid only because I was looking for interesting articles regarding aboriginal felicitude and mating habits, I ran across something more interesting.

Cave art. Old cave art from the days when Indians roamed all over the place without horses. What? Horses? We don't have any horses? We don't need no stinking *horses*! I don't understand how they got around without them. It was probably a very long walk to wherever they might be going. Maybe that's why they hung out in caves, waiting for the horses to show up.

What fascinated me, though, were the depictions of the parties going on. I saw cave paintings that were probably quite erotic for that time period. Since it was back in the BCs, there is no telling what the hell was going on back then.

Everybody dancing around a campfire cooking little nuggets of something on long sticks. It was too early for marshmallows to be around, so it was probably dinner. Looking closely, you could see Al in the ambience, or it may have been his cousin Peyote (the very first A&P by the way, soon to become a major chain down the road) because they were having way too much fun to just be swapping stories about what they did that day. The first of things you must learn about Al is that one of the favorite aspects of his mind is to never let the truth stand in the way of a good story. So Al had to be there, to liven up the atmosphere and lighten the mood, while waiting for horses to show up so they all could get the hell out of there. Even back then, it was evident that Al had a lot of potential and would put down a legacy that would become a legend. A dynasty, in fact.

Since I am a reincarnationalist, I think I recall that scene, and Al *was* there. He had a placard made from the hide of whatever they were having for dinner. It said *always*. It was a profound statement, but I don't remember why. I do remember Al taking charge of the social committee after that. And though it was tedious at times, Al kept us all in stitches, with tales of places he'd been and the mischief he could instill in even the simplest of characters, including famous people of whom we had never heard, who had no clue that they had been compromised. As I said, Al has a way of being everywhere at the same time. Where is he now? Give him a call, and he'll be there immediately. Trust me on that. Time and space have never been an issue for Al.

Speaking of which, in another space and time, not too long, cosmically speaking, after the horses showed up back at the caves with resupplies, another episode was unfurling as we speak.

The Universal Reality of Al

So since the Irish had the whiskey and the Russians had the vodka, being late to the party, the Meds were stuck with bringing the wine, not an un-sorry circumstance because the Middle East has some fantastic varietals. Just in case you don't know the incidentals behind the actual murder and mayhem Al caused at the time, I will tell you.

There happened to be a wanderer rolling around the neighborhood dispensing free wine and stuff at parties just because he could. They had no idea how he did it, but all you had to do was show up with a jug of water and presto-change-o you had a jug of wine! Plus, he delivered for free. A very interesting person and you can understand the following he must have had. Never a dull moment when he was around and never an empty jug. The lines were always out the door and around the block when he was on tour, and people even followed him around from town to town to listen to his stories and amazing feats of reanimation. He always threw in a bonus, usually a free eye exam, so at the time it was a hell of a thing. Free eye check, entertainment, and an open bar, just for fun! While everybody left those meetings whistling a happy tune, a lot of the congregants didn't need their eyeglasses any longer. As a matter of fact, there was a barrel outside the exit so the unneeded eyewear could be used by whomever had missed the boat. Talk about recycling, this guy was right on top of it, way ahead of the curve. He was something else, and he became annoying to the local merchants because he was seriously cutting into their profit margins.

Well, they could live with that for a while until they could organize a small business association that might be able to reason with the guy before things got out of hand. It was when he started to mess with their money supply vis-à-vis their clientele that things really got cooking. So you see, he *just wouldn't listen*! Learned lessons begin with listening to reason, but the guy was relentless, so a taut rein was imposed, but to no avail. There are some new souls in the universe that need a lesson to be taught before the first step is advanced. I guess this was one of those.

And the lesson to be learned was that you don't mess with other people's stuff just because you feel like it without paying the consequences. Drastic measures during drastic times, as it is said.

So one Friday night, after a long day of building shelves and an outhouse for his father-in-law, our wandering lawbreaker was relaxing with his buddies around the dinner table. Of course, they all ate and drank their fill, and with Al being present and accounted for and in such a glorious and exuberant mood, it was easy to forget about the troubles that surrounded them. Al is an easy distraction and quite likable, endearing in fact, in an abstract kind of way. Enticing but dangerous and easily seductive if you are not paying attention. Sometimes, Al and other souls I have met along the way have a common thread. Just saying.

Well, it being a Friday night and nothing else on the agenda for the rest of the evening, and spent from all the revelry, they all went their separate ways, making plans for the next day, looking forward to the next venue, which would be a show-stopper! Too late to realize that by not paying attention, they would soon all be in a world of hurt.

It wasn't until much later that the truth would be understood. Al was behind the whole thing, setting everybody up to take the fall by revving their engines from one side to the other. Al was at a great pivotal point here because he influenced both sides against the other and sat back with glee to enjoy the ensuing chaos. It was all about throwing a wrench into the works. It was the same force working on different sides for an amusing game of dice. It's all about having a good time and then reducing good fortune to gutter behavior.

On the one side, you have the wine merchants who also lent money to their clients at a "discount," while providing access to all manner of proclivities, some of which had never been thought of before then, and most of them still in vogue to this very day. Suffice it to say that these were very dangerous people to be dealing with and retribution was at hand. Plus, they loved Al more than life itself, because Al equals money, greed, avarice, and all the fun stuff that makes the world go round, and they weren't about to lose Al at any cost.

On the other hand, you have a wandering, good-hearted, well-intentioned soul looking for someone to lend a hand to. His story is that it just so happened that one beautiful day, there were some people having a party in their courtyard as he was wandering by, a wedding it seemed to be. They invited him in for a libation and were dismayed to find that Al had left the building. Realizing that he had just said hello to Al on the street just moments ago, the wandering fool decided to go fetch Al. He called for a couple of barrels of fresh water and a donkey (what great transportation modes they had back then) and took off after Al. Seriously, it was either one of the first of the Al-runs ever recorded, or it wasn't.

When he came back with Al, his wine-running accomplice, that is when things got into full swing. While the party was going on, he and Al built a makeshift desk in the courtyard (he happened to be a carpenter, Al being not so good with the mechanics of things, being left-handed and all, but he had ideas, which are a usually good thing), and offered to give free eye exams. It was such a big hit, he and Al hit the road as a traveling lecture/comedy/reality/optician program that would sweep the world. That's how the whole thing began. It was not his fault for spreading goodwill and free eye exams around. It was something everyone wanted, and he was good at it. Free stuff! What, is that wrong?

There were stories floating about how he hooked up with Al and where exactly Al came from, even though they all knew at the time, deep down, that denial was useless. Al was us! Much like soylent green, Al was destined to provide a sustainable level of clear-headedness that would transcend time and space-it didn't matter, because Al was always there, and everything was going to be all right. The level of clear-headedness always reflected the amount of time spent conversing with Al and the depth of topics involved. Little did anyone imagine in their wildest dreams that things were about to get weird.

The final straw was sipped dry; the other sandal hit the floor when it was discovered that the people who were calling themselves JC and the Wanderers were going to have a mega retreat (that is when you get a treat and then you get another one) at a garden in the hills.

There was a meeting held in the basement of one of Al's hangouts by the newly formed SBA, hosted by a kingpin of the local merchant's ass. Al, always there, was privately having conversations with members of the group and convinced many of them to follow their emotions instead of common sense. After a while, someone declared, "We have to get rid of this guy, for Christ's sake!" sealing the fate of untold millions of souls who were just standing in line waiting for free cocktails and eye care.

The rest is history, according to written records, but now you know the reality of Al and how devious and duplicitous he can be given a chance to play with you.

See, it was always Al, the greatest deceiver of them all, playing both sides against the other. He was, after all, in both camps at once, so it turns out that he was the true traitor in this situation, not some poor slob who happened to bring his own six-pack to the last supper before the big event.

I am sure that some have had problems with Al, but it's really not his responsibility to keep an eye out for people who want to abuse him. What is he supposed to do, not enjoy the circumstances of the situation? Bring it on. Al loves chaos, that's one of the functions of his reality, along with aid and comfort to other people in different modalities of distress. Al can be a help, a hindrance, a mensch, or an accomplice in evil deeds. He may also give wise council in times of stress, distress, or undress.

Witness a last experience in the fantasy/reality mode with this final short remembrance of sorts.

THE BIG ¥¥

It has been gleaned from ancient artifacts like wine cups, shards of clay jugs with Latin and Greek inscriptions engraved on them, and a whole lot of condoms (sheepskin can last a long time, especially if properly treated, and those Romans were really into treating well the things that served them).

The inscriptions on the sharded pottery revealed several different logos, but one in particular stood out. While some were inscribed with ads for local clubs and restaurants, this one seemed to be of some import because it showed up repeatedly in different trash heaps around the city after the big burn.

It was just one letter. A big double U, ¥¥. I know it should be two letters like two Vs put together or two Us put together, but they ran out of letters and came up with a single-segued dub/dub as a way to transition from new beginnings to a structured purpose; some had thought that it may be a good way toward communication without conciliation. So it is now. No telling what the inscription meant, but it was prevalent and quite popular among the masses. It turns out that many years after Rome's express to hell, there happened to be found a scribe's tablet. It was way up in the hills above Rome, near the ruins of an old distillery with alchemy involved. Al had put it into someone's mind at the time that it was imperative that someone needs to figure out how to turn olives into wine. After all, they were running out of a lot of stuff to use as aphrodisiacs, so they had to think of something else to mollify and modify the masses.

While Al and his cohorts were struggling to keep debauchery alive by making olive wine (how low can you go), they were depleting the olive oil production, forcing the fellow public to use outdoor grills. Their deep-frying days were over. This all led to the first pre-game tailgate parties at the Coliseum, where people crowded into the parking lot in their chariots. Some had little portable burners, that were one use only because you had to put what you wanted to cook on top of a small wooden pile of sticks that you could buy at concession stands according to burn time. A twenty-minute burn could cost as much as a beer in the ballpark today. But all you had to do after cooking is pick your shit up out of the fire and eat it. After all, you cooked it. The best part is there is no clean up. Ashes and dust don't amount to much, so let them blow away in the breeze. What a wonderful world, interesting times for very strange doings, and Al was always at the forefront of innovation when it came to fresh ideas. Sometimes the most destructive flags should never be unfurled.

So it happened one day that the conflagration that destroyed Rome was quite accidental, because as the games progressed in the city, there were people in close environs that could hear the cheering and oohs and aaahs that permeated their neighborhood. Plus, the smells wafting from the stadium reminded some of them of the times that they themselves were competitors in the big arena. While the residents were imagining their own participation vicariously by swinging imaginary swords and chain mail at one another, a great tragedy occurred.

It seemed that olives have a special consistency. You can make cooking oil that is really healthy for you (according to some), or for some purists in the "let's try anything" mode, it was a chance to explore new opportunities for Al to spread his wonders. Sure enough, since you could drink it (they came up with a 60 percent alcohol solution of fine olive extract that weirdly enough tasted like grapefruit) and cook with it (it made some really delicious crispy critters), it was inevitable that a worst-case-scenario episode was about to unfold.

It turned out that the pottery shards marked with ¥¥ were from vessels distributed throughout the city in all kinds of neighborhoods, and some that were marked §§ were also found in the general proximity of the source of the fires, there being a coincidental switching of the concoctions involved.

It seems that the ¥¥ was being used to fuel their personal fire, while basting their tasty treats in the §§, before slapping their stuff onto the grill. In their excitement over the frenzy being generated close by, some of the ¥¥ was inadvertently mistaken for the §§, and the place blew up into the inferno that is known today as the great devastation of Rome. It wasn't so great for the residents living there at the time, however.

Witnessing the chaos from up on the balcony of the distillery, the scribe, always the dutiful servant, was chiseling away taking notes of the massive barbecue that thousands of souls (in great pain and revelry at the same time) were participating in.

It was a mad, bad, sad, rad scene, so the scribe asked his buddy Nero to play a little something on his fiddle to accompany his history of the conflagration below. Nero, an accomplished violinist who despised being called a fiddler, took umbrage at the remark, but under the circumstances, umbrage was the least of his worries. The first one on his list was, *What the hell is going on?* The second was, *Why me?* and the third was, *What the hell did I get myself into?*

Needless to say, among those also on the balcony was Al, always present before, after, and during a momentous outbreak of downright calamitous circumstances that would kill you right then or you will survive to laugh about it later. As my dear sainted mother would say, "Foolin' always turns into cryin'." And she was never wrong in my experience. So there was Al whispering into the scribe's ear regarding the scene below while Nero was playing that tune from the Frankenstein (that's *fronconsteen*) movie where the monster was put at ease by catching butterflies while tuning in to the melody.

What Al was whispering became as loud as a shout because the scribe realized that what Al was telling him could change the course of history. His words were "Ne Veritus Obstet Fabulae Bonae," which translated from the Latin being used at the time was understood to mean "Never let the truth stand in the way of a good story." So he didn't.

Unfortunately, by the time the scribe's tablets were uncovered, being decades after what had come to be known as "The Rome Incident" in certain circles, it was too late to rewrite history. So the scribe was relegated to a footnote, but later records would show that the unknown scribe's mark turned out to be the mysterious ¥¥ and the fiddler's mark was §§, the fiddler being Nero himself!

After further investigation, it was determined that ¥¥ was in cahoots with §§, and the two of them owned everything from the olive groves to the B&Bs around town, not to mention the distillery, which they used to carefully cultivate an environment of happy and sad characters, depending on the mindset and proclivities of their target audience. It was all about marketing after all.

It is sad to say, but it must be said. Al's influence must be regarded as a harmful and helpful and inspiring and devastating companion to your reality. If you choose to entertain his camaraderie, please be advised of the conscious and conscience decision you are making. Al is no more of a problem in society than a firearm. Both are useful tools you might use in self-defense to fend someone off to avoid confrontations or maybe you are the instigator who just likes to see things burn down or the muse who portrays your ambitions as something you might get someday if you even try and avoid the pitfalls of self-aggrandizement. Al is not the killer here. The killer is your attitude toward those who love you and whom you love, after conversations with Al or during them. The problem lies unresolved, but Al is the truth behind it.

Protagonist, antagonist, muse, monster, instigator, facilitator, pacifier, jester, home-wrecker, and sometimes the decider of fate. Whatever Al is to you, it *is* you. You have Al's fate in your hand. In your head. Al is a reflection of who you are when your guard is down and open to all sorts of good ideas, but behavior once again rules the day where and when Al is concerned. It is all about paying attention. And taking things for granted is self-destructive at best.

So at the end of the fairytale episodes I have just reported, I maintain that between recorded history and the theories proffered from the above, there may not be as much distance as you might think.

Regardless of the truthfulness of the situations I've described, the concept becomes reality in the form of the following. This is why I decided to write this. As I alluded to earlier, this is a pretty close reproduction of the events that occurred in the past sixty-five years of my travels here. Normally, I would relax with the attitude that life sucks, then you die, so get over it. But something happened quite accidentally, recently, that smacked me upside the head and slammed me into the pavement. It was both an epiphany and a wake-up call that made me realize that I have to share my experience so that others may not traverse the same pitfalls without warning.

The story starts below but doesn't end until I do, so bear with me as I take you through circumstances that were very much in the controllable lane, but easier said than done.

CONVERSATIONS WITH AL

As a little background information, my mother was a beautiful Irish lass whose father came from the "Old Sod," as Ireland was and is still known, as far as I know or am concerned. I'm thinking it was probably the late 1800s when my grandfather stepped off the boat at Ellis Island. There he was, a five-foot-eight-inch ball of fire looking forward to making some fame and a little fortune along the way in the throes of the promise of the new and next generation.

Along with his newlywed, he arrived at "The Island" with a group of friends and neighbors and their families. It was a hearty clan that would stick together through thick and thin. Also, Al was along for the ride, so the voyage was made much more pleasant, although not as pleasant as the one on the Titanic, up until the end, of course.

As my grandfather's group descended the gangplank they were welcomed by loving relatives and friends awaiting their arrival with boisterous levity, as is the Irish way. At any rate, they all retired to a local pub and, along with Al "the instigator," commenced a storytelling marathon that lasted until the wee hours. They were all happy to be there and would go their separate ways very shortly, but it was good to seal a bond that would last a lifetime. And as always, Al, to take out the sting, had a few parting words that kept them all so enthralled that another day passed until the morrow when they finally said, "Enough of nonsense and let's get on!"

Most of the newbies had people waiting for them. Friends and relatives there to pick them up and take them to adventure in the northeast and yonder territories. But they all promised to keep in touch one way or another, and so they did.

As it turned out, my grandfather and the family located to Buffalo, New York, whereupon they proceeded to carry on in the new order of things.

You know, of course, that immigrants new to environs unfamiliar will tend to gather with like kinds, those with whom they feel most comfortable and relaxed while discussing politics and religious matters. The Irish were no exception.

So it was no surprise when my grandfather joined an "Irish Club" in one of the local pubs that reminded him most of home. Of course, Al was already there and a member in good standing, so my grandfather took an instant affinity for a friend from his past and was pleased that the connection lasted through the voyage. It was long but not unpleasant thanks to the wit and perceived wisdom of Al.

Time becomes memories, and it must have been in the late 40s when there was news of the passing away of one of the beloved group that first came over. It was unexpected and heartbreaking to those who loved him and whom he loved.

Word had it that his funeral was to take place on a Saturday morning, and not everyone had arrived from other places in time for the final wake on the Friday evening before.

So a few fast friends were sitting around the table at their favorite pub, mourning the loss of their dear departed friend, saddened by the fact that they weren't in time for the final respect due him. Yes, they could say a final goodbye at the site of his new "digs," but other ideas about a wake came to fruition after a conversation with Al, who by chance was in full sympathy mode.

After a prolonged palaver with Al and much storytelling and toasts, it was decided that "By God, we'll see him one more time!" So they drove down to the funeral parlor, where their old friend was safely ensconced in his forever "apodment," a place he would learn to embrace, while being embraced by it. In a while.

But first, they had to delay him from his premature departure and have a last hurrah! Knowing that their friend was behind locked doors did not discourage them from a little breaking and entering. After all, how much security does it require to protect dead people?

There weren't very intricate alarm systems at the time, so it wasn't very difficult to devise a plan. After realizing that they may get in trouble for criminal trespass or worse, it was Al who encouraged their spirit, for all at once declared, "In for a penny, in for a pound!"

It turned out that they didn't have to do anything but show up. The back window was open, and the smell of probably dead people was wafting through the darkened window. They went in through the window and viewed, with their army periscope flashlight, their friend for years relaxing in his finest attire, ready for presentation and burial the next day. They were all thinking that he looked a little lost. Kind of like he didn't understand the hubbub he was in. Why would he, of course.

With a little trepidation and much velocity, they hurried him out through the window, now darkened by shadows they didn't have. No matter, it was about giving their friend and fellow adventurer the proper dues him and to throw him "a party of a lifetime!" That was Al's line. Al is a funny guy.

So they took him, all dressed in his finest, and finely suppressed, laid out flat on his back on top of a "woody-wagon," you know the ones that had wood sides and door jambs that became a problem during damp weather. It may have been a Ford, which they used for toboganing, and they would put the twelve-foot toboggan on top all strapped down and have a romp at Chestnut Hill! It was kind of like surfing on snow, but there were eight others involved in the exercise aboard the wooden sled, and I'm sure there was fun in it because I have experienced it myself! An inherited trait that disregards danger and disturbs loved ones to the point of distraction. Or so I have heard.

No one ever said what actually transpired at the pub that night, not officially at any rate, but there were rumors that Al was the inspiration for the transpiration. Oh, really? The rumors actually considered were not really consequential or substantial owing to the fact that there were no consequences to consider that could be substantially verified to the point of prosecution. It was a private party, after all. So the local gendarmes turned a blind eye because some of the attendees were in fact members of both the police and the Irish club, and at least one of them was also an old friend of the dearly departed due to their shipmate-ship along with Al and the others. The reports of gunfire and prostitutes by some witnesses went uninvestigated by authorities because they couldn't investigate themselves now, could they? At any rate, fun was to be had, and by God, they'd have it!

As the story was told to me by other relatives, my grandfather apparently (along with his mates) propped their dear friend belly up to the bar (he was already stiff at that point of his little adventure), put a cigar in his dead fingers, along with three fingers of Jameson's neat at his elbow. His favorite libation.

Old stories were swapped, jokes told at other's expense, and a general levity permeated the atmosphere. Everyone had an excellent time until near dawn, at which time they figured the party was finally over and they should probably take their buddy "home" before daylight.

It was still dark when they returned their friend to his next stop, the next to last he would make forever. The last would be down the road to his "new sod" in a couple of hours, and everyone present tipped their hats, said a silent prayer, and slipped back out the window that still smelled like probably dead people. They left the window open.

Lo and behold, when the gatekeeper/mortician arrived that morning for final roll call and inspection before interment, he opened the casket and couldn't decide whether to laugh or cry or scream! So he did all of them.

There before his eyes was a man, just the night before, he had "dressed to kill" for his burial, all dolled up and nowhere to go. This guy was a disaster! His hair was messed up, and his tie was missing (it was found later wrapped around one of his private parts). There was cigar ash on his lapels and what appeared to be whiskey stains on his shirt front. Not to mention the lipstick on his collar and around his trousers' zipper.

The finishing touch was, a kind friend had sweetened up his lips into a lovely faint smile with lipstick, a different shade than the one on his collar, or his zipper for that matter, which matched neither one. Interesting. His smile was kind of like that in that famous painting of the woman with the mysterious look. Satisfied?

The other odd thing was that for all intents and purposes, he may have been an early member of the ATF, because he reeked of all three: alcohol, tobacco, and firearms. Anyway, the funeral was delayed for repairs (how long does it take to repair a dead Irishman?), and the mourners did what they always did in times of grief and distress. To the pub!

Of course, Al was there and pretty much holding court. Another celebration of life! There was hearsay about this and that, but everyone knew that Al was behind it. He was the instigator behind all the shenanigans, but it sure was worth it. If it weren't for Al, they would never have taken the risk, but the fun they had would be forever remembered.

That missive was a memory of mine from a memory of someone else's, so I can't vouch for the veracity of the tale, but it is an amusing anecdote in my historical reverie, like I almost remember it.

Sometimes myths and legends and truths have a way of commingling to the point that all three become a common knowledge when passed on by mouth to ear. While Al's favorite saying was "Never let the truth stand in the way of a good story," I kind of put this in the believable column, just because it seems like something I would do, and it just makes me smile.

I think it's interesting how conversations with Al can be totally fun-loving with a "no harm, no foul" attitude. But sometimes Al can have a darker side. Like the times he tried to kill me. I can't really blame Al for trying to kill me. I didn't know that once your perception as a teenager can be influenced by a higher power; it changes your point of view on certain things that should make sense, but sometimes you question what common sense is when it just escaped your mind. I got too involved with Al too soon or not soon enough, because not understanding access versus excess in your life will get you a little on the darker side where things aren't settled until the end. Perhaps one day you will find a companion with whom you enjoy lively conversation and can relax around. And believe it or not, Al will probably be along for the ride one way or another.

AL IS A FUN GUY

I guess I became aware of Al at a very young age, maybe nine or ten, just when you start to get your head out of your ass and begin looking around past your own little world. Al became kind of a staple in our house when party time came around. Every time we had company over for a weekend grill or to watch a ballgame—football, baseball, basketball, hockey, whatever—Al was always present.

Sometimes, when friends and relatives would come over, we would all gather in, you guessed it, the kitchen, where always you will find the heart of any home. That has been my experience, at any rate. The kitchen was fairly large with an island cupboard in the middle. Large enough that several people could stand around and shoot the shit but far enough away from each other so as not to pick up stray fisticuffs if things got heated. Some people picked their positions regarding the temperament of the antagonist, choosing to stay out of easy reach in case things went wacky. I was one of those who would step back and observe the interaction, glad to be in on the excitement but reluctant to participate in any harmful activity. Some may think I was pussified, but I maintain that I was being prudent, for of what purpose is a wounded witness. He started it!

Really, though, they were mostly fun-loving adventures into the whimsical, with Al leading the charge. We would set up a couple of jugs on the counter (like I said, it was a pretty big island) and talk about all matter of things. Just for fun and conversation. Very rarely a dull moment. That is probably when I first heard about the fun and frivolous ancestry I was in possession of. They left out the part about the famine and what went on over there to drive them west to new beginnings. Potatoes? Who needs potatoes? We don't need no stinking *potatoes*!

Anyway, life went on as it usually does because what else is it going to do? As I got older but not really that much wiser due to the fact that at eighteen years into it I was about to make an error in judgment that could have ended mine in a heartbeat, so to speak. More on that will follow shortly.

So it was that I cultivated friendships in college who seemed to be on the same wavelength as I was at the time. You know, the thing about like-minded people attracting each other. Of course I was part of the group dynamic, and always at the parties was Al. Not quite the center of attention, but it seemed that everyone would stand around in line waiting to have a conversation with Al, no matter how brief. It turned out that due to varying aspects of their childhood, some of my friends were more conversant with Al than I was at the time. I tried to make up for my lateness to the party by paying closer attention to what was being said or, not knowing that Al's influence and persuasive abilities could confound and bamboozle any given soul, should always be taken with a grain of salt.

Looking back, as I think about it, Al was a great companion. A good friend to us all. He was with us through the teenage years. You know that being eighteen in 1972, there was a lot of angst involved during that time. The draft was in its last rotation and Vietnam loomed very large on the horizon, and if your number came up after a certain troop replacement number, you were free to explore other life opportunities. Whew! Was that ever close, mine was 321, and I selfishly thought that there but for the grace of God go I. So for those of you who sacrificed your lives and livelihoods, I thank you for your service, and God bless every last one of you, in this life and the next; eternal gratitude awaits.

But interacting with the people I ran into at the time almost always reflected a sense of humor and optimism regarding current events, Nixon being the butt of most of the jokes on late-night TV. Al was no slouch when inspiring diatribes were needed to fuel the fires of passionate discourse. You go, Al! It was a very interesting and volatile time to be almost out on your own, kind of like idling for takeoff. "But I've never done this before!" That type of thing. So Al helped us get through, even though some would not make it due to various reasons. Things do happen after all.

One evening (very early morning, actually), after deep conversation and celebration of my birthday with Al and my mates at our local watering hole, I decided to hit the road. It was closing time after all, and Al was wearing me out, with the parting shots and birthday jabs. Since I wasn't seeing double, I figured I was okay to drive. In other words, I didn't have to close one eye to see only one of what I was looking at. Good to go!

I jumped into my mother's car, which she had let me borrow since after all, it was my nineteenth birthday and I really, really would behave myself. I should have felt ashamed for lying to my mom, but at the time, I thought I was pulling a fast one. But it was a special treat because it was brand spanking new and very cool. A beautiful cherry red with a black vinyl top, a 1972 Cutlass SS Coupe! An awesome ride, for sure (we added the 8-track for max tunes). One of my brothers had put in an outrageous sound system with woofers, tweeters, reverbs, and all the things necessary to destroy your eardrums. If you weren't careful, you could blow out the windows. Pink Floyd? *Fogettaboutit!*

So I decided to cruise by the old alma mater (I had just graduated high school the year before!) for nostalgia's sake on the way home. I turned into the neighborhood where my old high school was located, and there was a very nice meandering road that went by the campus. The road in front was set up in wide turns, like an elongated *s*, a slow and wide two lane that is quite lovely during the day, with really old oak trees guarding the sidewalks. It's especially beautiful in the fall when all the trees turn into living fire. But at two in the morning, it seemed a little foreboding, and so I hesitated for just a moment. After a brief discussion with Al about logistics (Al was next to me in the passenger seat acting as navigator and advisor), we came up with a plan.

It appeared that with the precision of the trajectory and velocity involved, along with some nerve, I might add, there was a lane of opportunity. Since the road was a pretty wide street and the curves went zig and zag, we figured that going straight through the flue was the best option, because it really was way too curvy to negotiate the turns without hitting the curbs. So as Al says, "In for a penny, in for a pound!" I spotted a really old oak at the end of the run, probably about a hundred yards away, with a turn to the right just before the tree. So we're talking about maybe twenty feet before decision/reaction time at the end of the run. If I aimed for that tree, I wouldn't have to even steer, like autopilot, until the end. Having a good shot at this, Al and I took the controls and decided to do some reckless conduct.

It was an excellent plan on Al's part because sure enough, we enacted our "quickest way between A+B is a straight line" concept, and it was working! This was probably on account of the fact that the lateness of the hour (or earliness of the same) described the conditions of the traffic at the time. There was nobody around!

We proceeded at a precipitous rate (25–30 mph), and the first little curve on the passenger side came close and then faded like a serpent dodging my tires in my side-view mirror. Then the curb on the driver side arrived and disappeared in the same fashion. It seemed that I hit the "sweet spot," and I cruised past the last snake on the right until *bam!*

Oh my! That must have really hurt! Thank God I don't remember it. It was a pretty good shot, though, because I hit the tree smack dab in between the headlights. Talk about focus! It's the blink of the eye at the end that throws your timing off.

There was my target, my own private three-foot-wide oak tree sitting where the 350 hp engine was supposed to be. The engine wasn't in the engine compartment because it was sitting next to me, between the driver's seat and the passenger's seat, where Al was supposedly "navigating" from. The transmission was still working as far as I could tell, but I couldn't actually see it since it was in the back seat. At about 30 mph, I'm afraid I shaved a few years off that poor old tree's hide. Counting rings as years, how many rings in a tree year? If it's one, then I probably hurt myself more than I did him, but I must apologize for my reckless behavior. I caused harm to an innocent tree, standing guard over a peaceful neighborhood, all the while there you are gallivanting all over the neighborhood doing God knows what until the wee hours, and what did you expect, hugs and kisses? (That's my mom, ain't she cute?) After the expected loving remonstration, that is exactly what happened. Hugs and kisses and undeserved forgiveness, but that is what moms are for, right?

I did get a little banged up myself. Nothing broken but promises of good behavior, which probably hurt my poor mother than the physical plane I was on. My brain was a little addled, and I had deep lacerations under my jaw and my knee where I must have smacked into the eight track while kissing that oak. That used to happen during make-out sessions back in the day, but this was a bit more violent. One thing to remember is that if Al is involved, be careful of the things that you want to recall.

So when the paramedics arrived, it turned out that I was in the passenger seat. How I got to the passenger side was kind of, and still is, a mystery. How did I get from the driver side, where I was negotiating a slalom-less slalom ride, into the passenger seat where I ended up? The first responders thought that there was someone else driving because I was on the passenger side and it would be near impossible for me to "get over the hump," so to speak. From the driver side to the passenger side was a real hurdle, and since I don't recall the specifics, I can only assume that adrenaline is a crazy thing, and I squeezed over before passing out.

Since the driver-side window was broken and the door couldn't be opened due to the crunchiness of the situation, they insisted that someone else had to be driving and used the broken window as the escape hatch to freedom, leaving me behind to suffer the consequences of my folly. So to think of something, I named a good friend of mine at the time (at the time we were conversing with Al, and what a time indeed!) as a kind of a "Give me time to think of a better one" type of maneuver.

He, of course, denied the whole thing after having been dragged out of bed at 4:00 a.m. and explaining to his mother (with whom he was living) and the police that it couldn't have happened, and his mother corroborated the story. It turns out that when my friend arrived at home, after leaving me, he and his mother played gin rummy with Al until around three or so. That Al is not only a fun guy, he gets around. While they were playing cards with Al, I was wrestling with a wayward engine and thinking of a conversation I had with my dad, from eight years before. I was eleven at the time, and he was thirty-nine, and I was worried that he was not going to make it to forty, which, sadly, he didn't.

So I was recalling the last time I saw my father alive, not really in a flash like you would imagine, more of a rolling clip of a last conversation. It seemed that I had plenty of time to ruminate, since at three or so in the morning, there weren't many people awake to witness a smoking car sweet-talking your old oak guardian in your front yard! Good Lord!

Well, I had come home for lunch one summer day after a beautiful morning of running around with my friends doing kid stuff. Cowboys and Indians and all manner of artificial warfare took place, including World War II reenactments that the dogs of war would be proud of. It was essential for proper perspective for the years ahead, when wits and guile are finally ingrained and survival is what it's all about. But that morning, I was just having fun like you are supposed to do on a beautiful summer's day.

My dad was lying on the couch in our living room, relaxing and taking in some of the latest vinyl from Sinatra. I had come home for lunch that day because my dad had just returned (his last from the hospital that I recall) for a quick homeland visit.

He was very ill at the time, and unbeknownst to me, he would not survive the next year on this plane of life, but we would form a bond that has saved my life many times from that very day. My guardian angel, if you will. Upon my mother's request, I went to wish my father well and to say hello. I deep down realized it would also be goodbye, so I was a little trepidatious as I walked in. You know, the "reluctant shuffle," hands stuffed deep in your pockets while kind of observing all the accumulated detritus on the walls and the fireplace mantelpiece before daring to turn around and face my dad.

I say dared, because I didn't know what to say or do, so he pulled me close, and we hugged for the last time, and I believe that at that moment, we both knew what the other was thinking, and then he looked at me and told me that he loved me. Then he said, "Go out and play, son, have fun, and make good friends." Well, one out of two is not bad. Look at baseball, for God's sake—you bat .500, they give you a medal! But I at least had fun along the way, but probably not the intent of his words at the time, the more I think about it. I thank you for your advice, Dad, with sincere appreciation for our spiritual connection and love.

That was when my reverie was reversed back into reality and my whereabouts were confirmed soon after in the hospital. The ensuing visit with authorities went as well as could be expected. No charges for DUI were ever filed because it could not be proved that I was driving, since authorities could not believe_that it was possible for me to obtain the transverse position without assistance. Since they couldn't locate the mystery man and I was also totally clueless, due to the inebriatedness of the situation, it was chalked up to "oh well." They released me with regret and promises of retribution if I ever went near that tree again. I went by there anyway because the old Catholic guilt came to visit, and I had to apologize in person to the object of my failure to negotiate a turn and review the damage done. The oak looked a little worse for wear but once again on its way to recovery, although he never quite accepted my apology. No kidding.

I was happy that my friend forgave me and we laughed it off afterward. We both knew that it was Al behind the wheel, so no harm, no foul, right? And thank God for loving and forgiving mothers, who strive to keep their wayward children safe and sound, no matter how old it gets.

So it was, just me and Al, trying to get home from what may have turned out to be my last birthday party ever. We've had arguments before, but this was the first time (that I know of, at any rate) that he tried to kill me. I can't really blame Al for that one, though, because it was my fault for listening to someone who I knew to be dangerous or, at the very least, *could* be dangerous.

Al is a fun guy and can be a lot of laughs, but paying attention is a big part of Al's game.

Which brings into mind another small vignette. This is also a true story, witnessed by a brother, and if you ever get a chance to talk to him, he will testify to the stupidity and relentless ignorance that some people have regarding Al and all his activities. Move ahead. Pay no attention to the man behind the curtain—he's only a distraction.

ACES AND EIGHTS

S o it was a little down the road that I discovered another fork there that I had to take to the left or right, so being right-handed, I took an immediate left, to avoid a weeping willow who wanted to occupy my space. I look back now, but I didn't then because I was into adventure still and being in my late twenties (I guess around 1982 or so), nearing thirty, and still acting a fool, it was all in the rearview mirror.

The way of the world, or so it seemed at the time. Until I ran into something called "the hillbilly *affect*." It's a little different from "the hillbilly *effect*" in that the former denotes a person who relishes the hillbilly look and would like to come across as a hayseed over-all-wearing looking fellow with a wheat straw sticking out of his mouth and his hat in his hand, taking circumstances into account, of course. A harmless, haphazard, "aw, shucks" thing going on.

It did not occur to me then that there was another type. Something called the "hillbilly *effect*" that would almost make me wonder why I am still alive. My dear sainted mother would say something that reminded me of great sage-worthy prophets. "In case you don't know, I will tell you." There is evil out there and a gut check is better than a handshake any day of the week.

For some reason, it seems, I got hold of the latter, the "hillbilly *effect*" one. It was almost the ladder to hell. Well, I think I jumped a rung just by being in the wrong place at the wrong time for the wrong reason. While nothing is ever certain in your own little universe, one thing is. Paying attention is the most important thing you can ever do to protect yourself and the ones you love. That *does* include you and me, by the way. If you don't pay attention, Al will be there and attention will be lost for a while, taking a walk just wandering around, hands in his pockets whistling an aimless tune that almost seems familiar.

So I wasn't paying attention as I pulled up into my parking space at the apartment complex in which I was domiciled. Home. Ready to relax on a Friday evening after a long day at work. Maybe catch a ballgame on TV or read a little while having a little sippin' excursion with Al. I had the standard stuff furniture, Wal-Mart issue, certainly. Like a couch, TV, end tables (I remember having one at least), and a little kitchenette combo, you know the kind of stuff you carry around with you through the years whether they have given you problems in the past or not, you still can't say goodbye to them regardless of the memories, and they mean enough to you that you keep them around. Oh, there was also a queen-size bed with a nightstand and a lamp. All this stuff crowded into one big room was disorienting at first. Because the room was only 600 square feet, and that, my friend, you would classify as a one man's trash or treasure abode, depending upon the side of the tracks that divided your neighborhood while you were growing up at the time. To me, it was a tolerable arrangement because it was just me after all. I guess you pay for the location, because the apartment was on the second floor facing a very nice foliage combination with a creek within throwing distance of empty beer cans (you have to crumple them up so it looks more like a baseball than a kite). I learned this from my next-door neighbors upon my first conversation with them and Al (Al is always visiting neighborhoods and extolling virtues, values, and amazing stories, one of which almost cost me my life—again).

So I parked my car and headed up the metal stairs. The stairs ran up the right side of the building to a second-floor walkway that was open space on the right kitty-corner to the creek that my apartment faced.

Taking a left at the top of the stairs was the walkway to my apartment, the sun on the right, about ready to call it a night by slowly immersing itself in a purple, gold, pink, orange, and blue bath of dissipating daylight. Always a stunner. My apartment was only a couple of doors down the way on the left, with the creek flowing within beer can throwing distance underneath the sunset. It actually was a beautiful scene at the time, although looking back, it was just another beautiful sunset that I had witnessed at other times while living there, but this would be my last one in situ. I guess that is why I remember it in particular.

Well, as I turned left at the top of the stairs toward my apartment, my next-door neighbors were hanging out by the railing across from their door facing the foliage and creek beneath the setting sun. It was a mimic of my own place as far as aesthetics are concerned, except I was one door closer to the stairs in case of fire. Not that it mattered, because if you had a fire, all you had to do is hang down from the balcony and drop two feet. It's open air for crying out loud!

At any rate, my two neighbors were just hanging out, arms hanging over the railing, smoking and commiserating with Al, as I approached my front door. So I, being me, said hello to the two gents as I started to unlock my door.

Well, they invited me over to their side of the walkway, so I put my stuff inside my place and shut the door without locking it; after all, I'm right there, and this is not a walk-by neighborhood. It's a "You have to know where you're going in order to get there" type of place. So I wasn't worried about my belongings, as they were meager at least but functionally adequate and personal favorites; otherwise, they would be discarded as unuseful detritus, at my discretion. Not involuntarily at the whims of some passers-by.

After a while, as it was getting dusky and we were running out of ammo for the can tossing contest, they invited me in to parlay and play cards. It's funny how Al has the ability to extend a conversation without much substance. Sometimes it's as simple as wanting to have an interaction with someone besides yourself; other times it may be a feeling of danger or mystery that drives your curiosity to a new breed you haven't come across yet. I am guessing it was the latter. Another rung on the proverbial ladder to adventure; sometimes you gotta have faith.

Now I had only met these guys a couple of times before, since I had just moved in a few months prior and usually keep to myself. But they seemed okay, reminding me of those country folks you see in the *National Geographic* magazines about life in Appalachia and what inbreeding can do to alter a universe. At least at a local level.

They seemed harmless, in the "not paying attention" mode I was in. I didn't ask them if they were related because it was kind of obvious but not quite. Their demeanor was the same, so I assumed that they were raised in the same coop. Identical struts will give it up every time.

Lean, as if they had a hard life. They were about my age, maybe a little younger, mid-twenties, if I recall correctly, but looked older. The old adage "rode hard and put up wet" comes to mind. But you could tell that there was some kind of twitch in the atmosphere, that that kind of togetherness can only be borne from living together in the same pod for too many years. You know, the kind of people whose minds shift together without words so that their purpose becomes one and the same without having to realize the feedback between the two with a wink or a nod. An unblinking radar that hones in on human sap. 'Nuff said there.

But at the time, Al made me feel right at home so I and my two new buddies—let's call them Frick and Frack—and Al were just nickel and dimin' some poker hands, when the conversation turned to strange sightings in the woods recently reported in nearby Oklahoma, just north of someplace in Texas.

It became apparent, while playing cards and kibitzing with Al and my new FF, that something close to a thrill went down my spine and the hairs were all jumpy like "Let me get outta here!" all standing at attention like a rescue attempt was about to be executed. I kind of thought that the following would be an adventure, kind of like like-minded fun lovers looking for a story to tell your grandkids around a spooky fire past midnight in the woods with only owls and moonlight as the background ambience. Forget about the wolves lurking behind the bushes because the wolves are of no consequence. They won't hurt you unless they are provoked, and they are more afraid of you than you are of them. Say that to grazing sheep or those who are sleeping peacefully.

Well, it turned out to be exactly what I was hoping for but with an accentaigu. A small twist that makes everything copacetic and understandable at the end. The end, being nigh, was so far out of reach for me in my mind that only time would tell if and when the button will be pushed. Arrogance, denoting imperviousness to consequences, thought of or not, denote your value. You will get there eventually, but now was not the time to push it. And there we were, the four of us discussing UFOs, Bigfoot, and the scent of a big payoff if we could prove that Bigfoot exists. Excitement, enthusiasm, and Al! What a friggin' combo. As we were all in an "in for a penny, in for a pounding" type of atmosphere, we decided to take on the wild beast and at least try to capture him if we could.

An adventure, inspired by Al, was instigated right then and there that if there was a Bigfoot in southern Oklahoma, then by God and the USA, we were gonna take his hide and tack it to the wall of the nearest ASPCA and demand some answers!!

We were all fired up as Frick and Frack grabbed some checkered flannel shirts to cover up their tats and the wife-beaters they were sporting. It was pretty warm outside, but figuring it would be chilly in the woods when we got there, they brought along a couple pair of gloves and some other stuff. Like normal needed equipment to take down a savage wild beast who is stalking the neighborhoods and the woodlands searching for souls to ravage. They had a pretty long half-inch-thick rope, maybe a twelve-footer, a couple of flashlights, some duct tape, and handcuffs. Plus a machete and a butcher knife. Well, not wanting to be the only one unarmed, I ran into my own apartment and grabbed the biggest knife I could find. I was in a hurry for the expedition, so I didn't realize that my door was left unattended and unintentionally unlocked.

A custom Cutco that was about eight inches long and about three inches wide blade-wise was about to wreak havoc among hairy beasts, who have no rights except the privilege of being fodder to the fuel of righteousness. It was a real beauty, a very nice tool. So we dropped all the gear into the trunk of my new bud's car, a beat-up old four-door. I remember thinking (or not) that this was starting to look like the stereotype I mentioned earlier. The Effect one. Except these guys had most of their teeth, so I assume it's because they were only in their mid-twenties and hadn't had a chance to lose them yet unnaturally.

So Frick and Frack jumped into the front seat, and Al and I got in the back, me behind Frick, who was the driver, with Al sitting next to me, behind Frack. Since I was the designated navigator, I had the triple A maps that Frack pulled out of the glove box. Al was in charge of refreshments as usual and was happily dispensing good cheer to heighten the hilarity and party-ness that we were planning. It was really kind of fun, three idiots driving down the road all tanked up and ready to rock and roll us a Bigfoot. And have dinner at his expense. We all agreed that we hope he tastes like chicken and did you bring the hot sauce and if we brought doggie-bags with us. That was Al again, I'm telling you. A sense of humor? He's got it. That Al can bust balls with the best of them. I am sure it was an attempt at gallows humor, and we were laughing all the way to the first BF BBQ. That, my friend, was going to be the biggest, baddest first annual Bigfoot Barbecue ever! Since we didn't bring any camping or cooking gear, I figured we might capture him, sure. What—we had three against one, so not impossible. Plus, since we had Al right there with us to the end, I wasn't worried about no pussified people coming around. But it was way past midnight, around one or two, and there is no way we were going to have a BF BBQ in the middle of the woods. Well, a full moon did await, as did expectations.

And there was Al, a willing, witting, and wily witness and collaborator and instigator and cook. Someone said that Al could cook the legs of a lamb while it was still standing and it wouldn't notice it till his chops got cold. Hence wool socks.

We had plenty of fuel for car and man to run together in harmonious synchronization, one driving the other in a symbiotic relationship that transcended time and space. One energy propelling the ride to our final destination while the other driving our will to get there. It was thrilling and scary and nerve-wracking all at once. That friggin' Al, I am telling you, is a wild man, and he likes the edge as much as you do, and he'll push your button so fast it'll make your head spin, if you blink.

Well, while I was navigating from the back seat looking for the best ingress and egress to the final trap we were going to set for our newly now-sworn enemy, it occurred to me that they weren't following my directions. I had just blinked. While my head was in the map and not looking for road signs, I was giving them a sixty-minute recitation of the best way in and out, what kind of bait we should use. They laughed along with Al (the turncoat—nobody's side but his own) at the absurdity.

Bait? We don't have any bait! We don't need no stinking bait! All we gotta do, boy, is show up with you and let nature take its course. I laughed along with them as they were boasting that to be famous, we (meaning us, me included?) will be famous for having the first big-foot roast. While studying the map, I finally looked up and noticed the road was getting decidedly more desolate than the two-lane we were first on. The two-lane was still there, but the yellow stripe down the middle was fading and so was Al, and the pavement gradually turning into a slide instead of a ridge at the edges began to make me think that this was probably not a very good idea. It's funny what you think about and feel during those uh-oh moments. It's hard to describe, but "first encountered, never forgotten" would explain it for future reference. You will know it when the time arrives. Please have faith and hope you are ready for it.

I wasn't really ready for it because I blinked. But when the least expected happenstance in unsolicited real-time rescue was about to occur, I thanked my AG (*Angelus guardius*) for sending someone to pull me out of the fire—again.

A short mile or so after the yellow line became a narrow tunnel with big trees on either side, I kind of shyly asked Frick if, you know there, Fricky, are we there yet?

As they were mimicking my style of personal behavior (they never thought of me as a human being, only as a human bean, to be consumed with regular carbs like potatoes or rice or soylent green), they were howling to a different drummer.

We were about to turn into another trapper's hideaway when red and blue flashers lit up the dashboard from behind. As we pulled over, Frick and Frack looked at each other and mentally checked the box marked *Plan B*. That's when the brightest light I had ever witnessed exploded and lit up the car. It was so bright I could see that one of my shoelaces was untied. I also noticed that the trash that had accumulated during our little sojourn into the twilight zone was at my feet. While there was evidence of Al being there and actively involved in the pre-action, Al could not be found.

That didn't stop the local sheriff's department from taking us all "downtown" for a hoosegow sleepover. So I rode in with one deputy while the FFs got a different ride from the sheriff himself. The three of us were promptly and efficiently booked and photographed and given new accommodations that consisted a small room (6' × 8') with a steel door with no bars but a little window only large enough to accomplish mealtime access. A metal toilet/sink combo was screwed into the wall with notch-less heads, as was the sleeping platform. There was no bed, but you take what you can get. At least I had my own digs (just diggin' a different ditch, dog), and was grateful to be alive after realizing that the cookout they envisioned did include me after all. I was also glad not to have a roommate, so I could ruminate about self-destructive behavior and the toll it takes on people who actually care about you.

While the accommodations were pretty stout, it seemed a bit overkill in such a small town. It was not quite Mayberry, maybe a small step up from being run-down.

But they kept me there for the rest of the morning, what was left of it, and into the next afternoon.

My dear agitated brother drove up from Dallas to bail me out, about a two-hour round-trip, understandably pissed, but in a forgiving mood due to the underlying circumstances. (Thanks, bro, not for the first or last time.) On the way to pick me up in Hicksville, he ran into Al, who was looking for a ride to someplace else, other than the one he was at right then. So my brother, always an accommodating soul, took Al for the ride as he completed his trip, on his way to free a kindred soul.

After a protracted release procedure (it took less time to book me in than it took to book me out), I actually thanked the sheriff for arresting me and him personally for saving my life, although he didn't realize it at the time, or maybe he did. Maybe I didn't.

While my brother, being the pickup artist that he is (because he would always pick me up) was going through the rigamarole that was necessary for my freedom, the sheriff was telling me something I suspected but is one of those things that stops you dead in your tracks when realized and your heart does a very long beat, longer than normal, and you think, *I have been warned again, and I have to heed the warning and start acting like I give a shit about life and what the hell am I doing here wasting time and space in my head with all the trappings of a foolish reality?* That is in my mind—the "If it feels good, do it" thing is over and the "It's time to snap back to reality" mode kicks in, and you might be coming back to your senses. An epiphany of sorts, another lesson learned the hard way. But you are here to explore everything you can without killing yourself or someone else, never suspecting that just playing along also means paying attention.

After my brother and I were safely strapped in and were on the way back down the road traveled once too often in one twenty-four-hour period, I took the liberty of trying to relax, and with Al's guidance, I started to achieve that goal.

I relayed what the sheriff told me about those FFs who were my personal chauffeurs to hell. The Sheriff was explaining what his conjectures were regarding those two. He said it was a good thing for me I was stopped before our little bungle in the jungle, as he called it, because in his opinion, "Them boys was up to no good, son, and that's a fact." Well, shut my mouth, who'da thought?

His theory, which coincided with mine—after the fact, of course—was that our search for Bigfoot was going to come out a little different than the one I had envisioned. There were going to be Bigfoots, all right—four of them all stacked on top of me in the form of a heavy but cool blanket, tucked neatly at the corners to make sure that I was snug as a bug in a rug.

A little dirt nap was just the thing to solve a few problems, after all, and it wasn't going to be them who'd be sleeping.

Well, it turned out that Frick, who was driving, was still and behind the locked doors in Hicksville, because being wanted for numerous things that you have not yet paid for societally will hinder your whereabouts precipitously if apprehended. Plus he now has a DUI on his sheet, newly acquired. I never laid eyes on him after that.

Now Frack, the map bearer, was released pretty quickly after being arrested because he had an attorney on call (What is it with these guys?) who had him out before they were slamming me in for the duration of my hermitage program.

Frack had a pretty good head start, and since Frick was behind bars and unlikely to return anytime soon, it seemed that the Frick/Frack partnership had fizzled. Frack had a fourteen-hour get-along and a car that was no longer evidence of anything criminal because all we were really doing was driving around on a lonely road in the middle of the night in the middle of nowhere with a trunk full of killer equipment. If there was a story behind it all, it wasn't about to be told at that time. So while it was interesting in the suspicious/dangerous column of things within their bailiwick, the authorities declined to press it any further. It was a hell of an adventure and a pretty wicked ride and harrowingly close to the edge, at least in my mind, but against the law, it is not. You got a problem with that?

So I wasn't sure what to expect when we pulled up next to my car in the parking lot of my apartment complex. First I was surprised that my car was still there, but then I remembered that I still had my keys in my pocket, (having them being returned upon my release, along with my wallet and everything else that was in my possession at the time of my incarceration (all but my Cutco), and there wasn't any visible damage, so I was hoping that maybe Frack had taken off from Hicksville's coop and flew off to faraway places.

Well, Frack had flown the coop all right, but not before he returned to his place and emptied his apartment and took everything that the FFs owned of any value. So as the manager of the complex is asking me if I knew what the hell was going on, I am heading for my door, realizing, *Holy shit!* My bad, bad self. Another example of inattention getting the best of you. How many times are you going to trust people only to find that they want your blood, metaphorically or not? It's a rhetorical question, more of a metaphysical ponderance rather than an actual query, hence no question to be asked, so no mark. What? If you are with me on that, then we are both in close proximity to the wavelength I'm attuned to, give or take.

So with the bad scene that was in my head already, I wasn't totally surprised as I twisted the knob, and the door opened right up. Why not? Who needs a key when the door is left unlocked? As I walked into my place, my vacant stare was occupied by an empty room, my efficiency sufficiently reduced to a few possessions. Namely my bed, clothes in the closet, and personal stuff of not great monetary value. They even took my Cutco set of knives, minus the one piece still at the police department a hundred miles away. I doubt that they'll stop by to pick it up anytime soon. Me neither.

They must have had it planned out. The problem with Plan A was that I unwittingly (there were no wits involved in this episode) escaped the grinning fools, and I wasn't supposed to be coming back from our little midnight soirée. Who's the grinning fool now? Ahem.

While Frick is rotting his while away far away, Frack and his coop are still wandering around, creating havoc and mayhem with the best of them. Back up in Hicksville, they dropped the charges after all. I was actually just a passenger not in possession of anything more dangerous than my faculties, which weren't as sharp as my knife, which they kept. It was okay because the rest of the set is history, but in the end, I did recover some of my marbles, which I thought I had lost completely.

This whole adventure made me ponder about the vagaries of life and how it doesn't take much to get stupid very quickly. It's all about paying attention.

A Peaceful Presence

After I pulled my head out of my ass for the nth time, I found that it was decidedly time to give up bad behavior in favor of something a little more family-friendly.

Being in my early thirties during the mid-eighties, I was about ready to proclaim the party over. At least the crazy stuff. Getting married, raising children, being gainfully employed, and having a house in the suburbs with two cars in the garage and a built-in swimming pool in the backyard. A sweet little patch to call my own and my own little family, snug as a bug in a rug. Another wild dream or just a wish.

While it took several years to accomplish all that stuff and a lot of sweat (and sweet at the same time) equity, and pain sometimes associated with tense situations, it appeared that the visualization of my situation had come to fruition.

Life actually *was* grand. Of course, Al was a big part of all of our lives. Not that there was any cause or effect per se, more of a permanent invitee to everything social. What with birthday parties, cookouts, sports-watching events, and just general merrymaking stuff that makes the world more fun than drudgery, Al was one active hombre.

So now, the kids are grown and leading lives of their own someplace else while you and your spouse are about to embark on a different life together. Things start to slow down a little, and you're nearing retirement, but still working at a job you love with people whom you love and respect and you feel it in return.

Instead of just partying with Al on the weekends and holidays, special occasions, whatever, you decide to start giving him a buzz just to see if he's bizzy. You know, no special occasion, just checkin' in, see what's up.

You're still working full time, and everything is copacetic, all cylinders humming nicely, and there you are getting ready for a milestone sixty years of survival in the wilderness of the human wonderland. Almost there. You might have daily conversations with Al, but they're always short and to the point but never hurried.

It doesn't seem to affect anything in your daily life except your attitude toward it, and it seems like the perfect cruising altitude, so you maintain your daily talks with Al while still being a competent and confident member of society. Plus, you are having fun, so no harm, no foul, am I right? What, is that wrong? Not on my watch.

Not yet anyway.

WAKE-UP CALL— EXPRESS MODE

D id you ever have anyone play a practical joke on you? Like they know you are planning on sleeping in after a jovial evening with Al and friends, and what the heck, there's no work tomorrow, so you're taking self-indulgence one more step, with a smile on your face. Maybe someone, could be anyone, might be a little ticked that your attention was being distracted by something that annoys them, and it might be time to get a little payback. So they set your alarm (*loud!* The British National Anthem!) for the most inopportune time, like maybe a couple of hours into the REM mode.

Then they stand back when the alarm goes off just to see you jump and laugh with glee as you stumble for the snooze button. It's kind of like that in a way. Only more intense. Sometimes you can sense the chaos headed your way, and like the other times, to avoid repeating the same thing twice, you decide to get there first, since you're going there anyway, and after all, it's a race, isn't it? Destiny and fortune may cross each other's paths throughout the journey, back and forth, but they are not necessarily a reflection from the same pool. Get some rest because chaos awaits.

I guess the real thing started the morning of a scheduled doctor's appointment. The evening before, I also had an appointment. This was with my old friend and companion for almost as long as I can remember. During our short but informative conversation, I put forth my concerns regarding my upcoming exam. Al assured me that we had this "in the bag." See what I mean? Al has a way of calming your nerves and rattling them at the same time. It is uncanny, but so it is effective. It didn't matter that I stopped taking my blood pressure meds six months ago because I exercise and my heart was in the right place, and invincibility was still in my active file wrapped around a strand of wacky DNA that just would not let go! Plus, Al was keeping me healthy with our daily conversations even without my blood pressure meds. And I hadn't had the flu in years.

I was feeling a little punk that morning, however, more than usual, as I entered the doctor's office to present myself for inspection. The receptionist saw me, and the shocked look on her face suggested that she was about to scream! I quickly turned around to see what kind of ugly evil could possibly create such a visceral reaction, hoping it didn't follow me in unawares. Since there wasn't anybody there, I immediately realized that the source of the commotion was only me.

As I was standing in the lobby, they started to arrange for an ambulance and took me someplace to take my blood pressure. Since my heart was making my shirt flutter like a flag in a stiff wind, I knew it was pretty high, but I forget the numbers. I just remember someone yelling stat and then an ambulance ride to the nearest ER.

I was admitted and put under observation, which I think really means "Park him here if he's not about to kick the bucket and put a flag not a tag on the toe." A little yellow one that signified the level of panic that should be involved. The flags were a pretty good idea actually because the doctors didn't have to look at your chart to find out what's going on. Red is for "Hurry up," the yellow one was for "Relax, he's not going anywhere—we'll get to him when we run out of red ones," and green is "Why is this person here taking up space when time is of the essence immediately to the people who need it most?" You know, since time and space are inexorably inseparable (at least as far as we ken right now), it really would be helpful if you occupied a space and time other than the one that possibly may save someone else's life and excused yourself from the line. Try helping by nixing the crying wolf.

They ran a few tests—you know, the usual, I guess. EKG, CT, and the old GI Joe, which was a concoction that consisted of a chalky milkshake looking thing that I really didn't have the stomach for. Something they called "The Full Monty," and I could smell popcorn and hear anticipatory laughter in the background, and so I was a tad apprehensive. But I drank it, struggling to choke it down so they could witness the psychedelic kaleidoscope that is my digestive system, working its way through my intestines, one after the other, first the lower, then the upper and around the bend, and then the finale, which I imagine was pretty tough to watch. I understand that if you put certain dyes in the interactive but harmless, solution of GI Joe, there is quite a show to be had. Living color on a real-life journey. I wanted a copy, but they claimed they don't keep them. They are not for sale either. I checked. If I find out there are any bootleg copies out there, please be advised that I am already wise to you.

Well, I spent the morning there, starting from around ten that Wednesday morning until they released me at around nine that same evening.

During that time of bed-riddency, I was in an open ward with about twenty beds around the perimeter, all separated by pale green sheets that might have instilled peace, calm, and harmonious attitudes, except that you are in a friggin' hospital and there are a lot of half-dead people walking around. Deal with it.

There was also a cluster of beds in the middle around the nurses' station, an oasis in the middle of another flu season, most of them contained patients with the red flags on their toes. That meant that as the reds turn to yellows, my chances of getting out of here quickly increased. They left the green ones out in the hallway, figuring they'll probably get tired of the inattention and go home, for God's sake! I started taking note of the change in colors of the toe flags, waiting for the steady beat of yellow.

Since I was on the perimeter, I could look through a very narrow tunnel of hospital green to view passers-by. People were walking back and forth past in front of my little envelope of misery, some wearing masks, some with walkers doing "the sad, sick shuffle," one slow, tentative step after the other—*thump, scrape, thump.*

I remember thinking, *Why are all these people here up and walking around spreading germs and whatnot to people who are already sick or going to be that way soon? Where are they going?* I think they call them floaters, now that I think about it. That's when you're in the hospital for a long period, so to get your exercise, they hook you up to an IV on a pole for nutrition and balance and send you out into the hallway half naked to wander around and hopefully stay out of the way.

Yeah, floaters. I remember going through the same routine a few years back when I was recovering from something else not related. I'm not sure if that's what they were called or not at the time, but the purpose remained the same. Spread the ongoing flu by personally airmailing it to everyone you pass in the hallway.

Anyway, what's that phrase, "dead man walkin'?" It's like that. They were a meandering deadly bastion of germs, but what are you gonna do?

At least there was a TV in each little tube. Thank God for *Law & Order* reruns. I had seen almost every one of them previously, some of them on their original air date, but they were always entertaining because of the lighthearted banter among the seasoned detectives, who were in and out of their scripted insanity/reality lives.

What a world, but it was time to get back into my own private, unscripted insane/nightmare/reality/ program, an unpleasant surprise and something that I wasn't expecting but turned out to be a blessing in disguise. Again.

Another lesson to be learned. Which way? Pick a fork, not a spoon. The hard way, of course. Well, after binge-watching L&O all afternoon and having one of the hospital's mysterious entrees for dinner, it was time to unveil the results of the matinee's presentation of the gutless wonder review that was my premier debut. I say gutless because a couple of years prior, I had an issue with colon cancer and had part of the ascending one removed, leaving a shorter road to freedom for the rest. Sometimes liberty involves removal from a situation, and it was deemed worthy of sacrifice to create a quicker route to the outside and freedom at last for the compressed. That's when my floating days, as an active participant, took place.

Whatever, I was about to see what was up. Since I was, and awaiting with bated breath the termination of my little side-track adventure, it turned out to be a bit of good news. Clean as a whistle. As a matter of fact, one of the nurses told another attending that when she blew up my ass, all puckered up, she could hear a soft moan of delight and aspiration (they thought I was still unconscious). It was inspiring, to say the least. So much for the bated breath.

Since all the tests were negative, despite my performance, I certainly took that as a positive. I wanted to personally thank the puckerer for the whistle that saved my world and specifically the tune it inspired. Unfortunately, her lips were sealed and couldn't be reached for comment.

Well, what is important to remember, for future reference, is the "clean as a whistle" part, the negative results after the testing part. After re-prescribing my absent meds, and an admonition that "This is why you don't go off your meds without a doctor's advice!" I was released on my own recognizance. That parting shot would turn out to be ironic and prescient simultaneously. Something about synchronicity, not exactly coincidence but a cosmic comeuppance in a way.

SAFETY IN NUMBNESS

I arrived home that night around 10:30 p.m., after retrieving my car from the doctor's office where it was left that morning. My home is a small two-room walk-up from the side arrangement that terminates at a T, at which point on the right is my place, the rear end of a one-hundred-year-old house. *Quaint* is probably a better description than "quality it ain't." Upon opening my front door, you would walk into my bathroom if you took two steps forward. You had to position the doors so that they could be arranged in a maze-type thing so you could enter the room on the left, which is immediately right there. You just have to pay attention, but you get the hang of it. So closing the front door, the kitchen is also right there, since there is no hallway. You have to walk about a six-foot diagonal alleyway cluttered with household kitchen stuff on both sides to get to my bedroom. There are a couple of windows on the left above the sink that would be sorely needed very soon. At the end of the short trip is my eight-by-fifteen-foot "man cave," a term I really don't care for, but it probably describes it as well as anything else. It's where I eat, sleep, and entertain myself, so whatever. But it also had a couple of nice windows, one of which contained an AC unit, always a comfort.

The reason for the logistical tour is to describe the torture chamber I would stumble and crawl back and forth through on my journey to hell and back. While so far this has been a fairly light-hearted account, I have to warn you that this is going to seem to be a little bit much, even for me, and I was there. So if you think it's over the top, read it with one eye closed, but understand the truth that is here, because something unexplainable occurred while going through what was later understood to be an acute alcohol withdrawal syndrome—full-blown episode without any medical attention. It seems it can be a very dangerous situation, even deadly, I am told. Well, I don't have to be told jack because this here is a firsthand account, practically blow by painful blow with razor-sharp remembrances of something I will never forget until I get it out of my system. Maybe help if I can. That's kind of the point of all this. I lived through it to tell the tale and warn people to just pay attention to what you're doing. I am not sure if it's ever been captured live on tape anywhere because there is no way you could film it from start to finish without halting the process.

The circumstances would be so dire that you would have to render aid to save the subject's life. With all the fever and convulsions involved, someone would surely jump up and say something like "Hey! We gotta knock this guy out!" Something along those lines would be appropriate. Not knowing if the subject would live or die might be problematic for a legitimate research project and closing down the experiment with some outside influence (like, Hello! Medical Attention!) would negate the value of the exercise. So, I'm thinking that there probably is no tape, since it wouldn't fall into the fun to watch category unless you're into that type of thing. Please-God! Maybe there is, somewhere. That is a pretty scary thought.

I now wish that I had the foresight to perceive the value of recording something like this, if only for the research and insight it may provide. However, at the time it happened, I wasn't really sure what the hell was going on. So you are just going to have to trust me when I tell you about this little trip that I took without the aid of any hallucinogens, synthetic or otherwise. Neither was Al anywhere in residence. It seemed that I was going to be my own first responder, going into an unknown situation with no backup, no medications, no tie-downs, no intuition, and the wits that I had were about to desert me.

So the things that are unexplainable will be left unexplained, although I have conjectures to proffer that may involve the need for further study than I have the wherewithal to present here. Is there a doctor in the house? Maybe you could look into it. It's a curiosity about how things work and why certain organs interact with each other, like knowing when to help a brother organ out to save a life. It's kind of like a symbiotic osmosis behavior, akin to bailing out a foundering boat, where shipmates will die trying to save the other, while expecting the same concern for each other in return.

It never occurred to me before my episode about how much we take for granted the amount of abuse a body can and will take before things fall apart. Or when that might occur. I am sure that paying attention is the key, again, here. Well, the other key is to keep your prescription protocols up to date.

Apparently, you had better add Al to the list of your prescription meds, self-prescribed or not, if it's a daily dose that you're taking. It doesn't matter what the dose is, but Al should have a special warning of his own. Something like "Make sure you don't skip me for over 36–72 hours straight or I will really hurt you." That seems about right. I guess my number was around 40. Still in the window, one leg out and the other too far in to turn back, even if I wanted to.

Too late. After a fitful sleep, I aroused myself from a worn-out feeling of being tired, a little out of sorts, kind of like hunger, but not feeling hungry, like I couldn't eat it if you put it in front of me, afraid to choke on it. I had felt it before, like a déjà vu experience, usually associated with my disassociation with Al, as time goes by.

So around 11:00 a.m. or thereabouts, I found myself with that feeling that I should probably eat something, since all I had to eat recently was that hospital entrée at around five last afternoon and the cup of GI Joe that was used for entertainment purposes only, apparently, because I was about to undertake a huge reorganization of my own GI, no *joke*.

So to satisfy my perceived hunger pangs and out of curiosity toward whether it would stay down or not, I made an egg sandwich, and as I started to chew, I realized immediately that this was not a good idea. After not being able to get past my esophagus even the smallest bite, I actually had to spit it out. I tried to drink a little water to whet my whistle and managed to sip about a half of a cup.

At the time, I thought that I might have contracted the flu that was running rampant at the time. After all, I just got out of a place packed with diseased, disoriented people wandering around aimlessly regardless of the consequences of their exercise program.

That half cup of water turned out to be the cork that popped a serious pressure point that must have been compressing for a long time because I instantly felt nauseous, like I had to throw up. That's when the dizziness began, with an enormous swarm of little black dots, the ones you see in twilight while you're walking somewhere in the middle of someplace pleasant, and you are the disturbance that awakens them. Then vertigo dragged me down into an embrace that would keep me captive for several hours. It didn't keep me bed-bound though, because I had to get up and walk around, pacing every step like it was the last one I was going to take, vertigo or not.

There was nowhere to go but from my bedroom, through the kitchen, to the bathroom, and back (Aren't maps a handy thing?). There I was pacing between two destinations, with no escape and nowhere else to go and nothing in my mind but the truth of the matter, which was that this was not the flu. The windows were open with the screens on to prevent bugs from entering, but at the time, it felt like that the air wouldn't dare. I couldn't get enough fresh of it, no matter how deep the breath.

I started sweating hot then cold, beginning to get cramps like something was plucking at my tendons, all throughout my body. I was right on the verge of the surge, but it just needed a little tickle at the back, so I tried the old tried and true method of annoying the appendage that's hanging there waiting for action.

That resulted in around the same amount of water that I managed to get down earlier, about a half cup. Nothing else, but I just felt like my stomach was ready to explode. My head was pounding, my heart racing, the flashes of hot and cold were so intense, I made it to the bedroom and hunched in my bed, in a fetal position, praying for relief, blankets on, blankets off, dizzy and disoriented. Just a minute or two was all it took to jolt back up and run to the bathroom. I got there just in time (isn't it always thus) to commence one of the most painful and violent episodes of vomitus eruptus that I had experienced in a while (one of them being a mezcal fest some place a long time ago—I ate the worm).

It took about three full stomachs' worth of something that I had never ingested to expel itself from my innards.

I'm looking at a couple of quarts swirling around before I even TKO'd the handle to send the stuff to the abyss that was awaiting. A vile mass descending down the reverse tornado depicted a mixture of what looked like chicken soup with no noodles or chicken but did have the usual greenish-looking oil that accompanies the mixture as it flows through the cascade, like a dangerous current.

Damn! That hurt. I stumbled my way back through the labyrinth that was my journey through the kitchen to my bed, still in a fever/chill and feeling dizzy and nauseous. Vertigo! Vertigo! Go! Go! Go! It wouldn't leave me for a beat.

Then something started vibrating, like a jackhammer in the distance that you can feel through the walls. Unfortunately, it was emanating from my own bones and accompanied by a spasm program that wasn't on the agenda. Mine, anyway. I developed these horrible contractions of muscles around my body, randomly chosen to confuse the situation, each short but intense outbursts.

While my head was pounding, muscles in my neck were contorting, then my legs, my arms, and chest kind of in sync with my back and abdomen and thighs in a pulsing rhythm that is akin to someone using your bones as a xylophone, while squeezing the breath out of you. I was in so much pain that I couldn't think straight.

All thoughts of any random virus were finally dispatched after the next bout of wicked nausea. As I lay there with the blankets on/off/on, up and down because I had to move to at least think of something else, my gut was filling up with something that I never ingested because my stomach should be empty but I could feel it from within, kind of like the surges that were squeezing my insides were trying to get the last drop from some internal sponge. A wringer for sure.

I went through this rebuild of fluid for about an hour or two—I can't be sure because I lost track of time. It was starting to become a very long afternoon. Pacing back and forth between my bed/bath/bed to keep some action going so you just gotta move to survive!

Finally, I knew it was about comeuppance time because of the last time, and I was looking forward to the relief I would feel after the fun was over but didn't really want to go through that again. Not that I had a choice in the matter.

Since I was expecting it, I made it in time to make sure I hit the target, because the first one made quite a mess, being first try and all, you know. What gruesome concoction came up looked decidedly like diarrhea (sorry)—thank God my olfactory senses were blown out because my head was about to explode. The thickness of watery chocolate pudding, the kind that mom used to make, lumpy as usual (sorry, Mom). Same amount of volume as the last, about two quarts, but the viscosity was much denser. I stayed there for a while, a minute or two, to make sure it was over, and waiting for that relief that you expect after an ordeal of nausea so intense. But as before, along with the fever chills and vertigo and the compressive turbulence in my innards, it would not leave me alone. The pain of that episode left me barely able to crawl back to my sweat-soaked bed.

I looked at myself in the mirror and witnessed someone who is in a lot of trouble, and it's not over yet.

Where is all this fluid coming from? How is it possible to expel something you didn't ingest? It seemed bizarre to me then, and it still does, because no one can explain it to me. Is it possible? I wondered if the bad vile running around my other internal organs was trying to send me a message and somehow wanted to get out of there and the other way was not available or up to the task at hand. Heading for Uranus might have been a constructive exploration, but at the time, I wasn't even ready for a moon-shot. So they planned on invading my system to get out through some sort of reverse osmosis thing that can seep through organ linings as a shortcut to daylight. Makes sense to me. Perfect reason to attack my GI and get out quick and dirty before all hell breaks loose. Mission accomplished? Not quite yet, because listen to this. This is the scary part.

While the nausea persisted and the cramps and with my head pounding to an unhealthy beat along with what was left of my heart, I became aware of something that I was always wondering about, while wandering about through the maze of the unstable reality that we are in right now (then and now are no different than the blink of an eye).

Am I going to die right now? I was thinking that this is probably not a good place to expire, since I was only thinking of doing the retire thing. New treads for a new travel. I mean, I love this place, and didn't want it to be defiled by having a dead body stinking up the place. I was a little concerned about clean-up activities afterward because I really didn't want to have anyone see the condition that my condition was in.

I knew then, deep in my soul, that I would survive this if I did not pass out. I wanted it to be over but at the same time I dreaded the ensuing aftermath. So I had a private mental conversation with Al, who always gives me a hard time. Well, for the most part, he's highly amenable. He wasn't there to bolster my vibes but certainly made an impression by his absence.

In a sarcastic frame of mind, Al is telling me a little story about angels and demons that will stay with you forever if you encourage their actions and let them play with your head. Either way, Al would not leave me alone because of all the years we had, conversations and soul-searching interludes when I asked for advice when there were no other friends around.

In fact, Al wouldn't let me go, having to want to pull me along the road without a wagon. I got it. He wouldn't let me pass out and wanted to inflict as much pain as possible for leaving him unannounced. He was pissed that I didn't call him like I usually do at the appointed time. Since I never had an appointed time, or so I thought, it seemed that the time to which he was referring was the last appointment involved. Like I said, about forty or so hours before.

Al was extremely aggravated that I dared to leave him without permission. He wanted to see me suffer only because he could, and enjoy the chaos conceived by his purpose as dictated, and to warn other deserters of the predicament you could be in if you are not paying attention.

It suddenly dawned on me that Al was just kicking my ass on general principle. What followed was a long internal struggle with Al telling me, "You don't leave me without prior approval."

"Got it, Al, you bastard!"

"You got it now! You got it now! Now you're really gonna get it!"

"Damn, Al, why are you picking on me! I thought we were buds. We grew up together for God's sake." I was whimpering like a child, on my knees by my bed, sweating and praying for some kind of relief.

"You thought you could use me for your own personal gratification for years and toss me out the window like a used beer can crumpled up like a baseball instead of a kite, but you never gave a moment's considerations to my expectations, and you were thinking that with a quick adios, there would be no consequences." It was a statement, like a dare, not a question.

(It reminded me of a divorce I went through once a couple of times before. I was a loser then too.)

Now a Strange Confluence in the Nautical Internal Atmosphere

I had to keep moving around to try and breathe because I started to have these pulsing effects that started to rake over my senses in a takeover mode. I looked in the mirror to see if I was still there and didn't recognize me. It looked like my head was about to explore another dimension, the veins and arteries standing out black against a white outpost. Eyes a fiery double-ought waiting for the trigger to be pulled. My mouth stretched in an ugly grimace, the ones that will depict a tortured soul, all of them. Man, this is gonna be the death of me.

As I was pacing back and forth through my short and more confusing and more disorienting maze between my B&B as time went on, it took unknown minutes (because there was no time or limits in my construct) to fill up my gut with a horrible consequence of reality. It's alive! I imagined that it was eating my insides in an effort to escape, and I was the only one standing in the way. Barely.

My whole body started constricting, all my muscles contracting. It would look like one of those bodybuilder people striking a pose. You know, really, really intense. But it wasn't voluntary, and I couldn't strike a pose because the pose was striking me. I could only adjust my posture here and there to alleviate the cramp site, so as to relax the spasms where the most powerful strings were being pulled, a master of the marionette move, perfect for plucking your strings, my buddy, Al. I had never experienced such a full body workout, and was afraid it was never going to stop, and about six and a half hours into it, I was feeling a little ragged. (Don't worry, it's almost over here, one way or another, and I'm telling you this now as I was telling myself then.)

As this was carrying on with the nausea, dizziness, gasping for breath, I could feel my stomach filling up with God knows what seeping in from all sides like a balloon about ready to burst. Finally, I knew it was time to expel this foul crap within me, because the stench of it was bleeding through my pores, and I imagined that it smelled like warm death, and since my olfactory senses were blown out, the fact that I sensed it was enough to trigger my response.

Which was to get to the head before my head got to me, because if I thought about it, I wouldn't get there in time. Call it a gut reaction.

Well, I guess that the third time pays for all concept was active in this case because I was about to witness something that I still don't understand, and will never forget.

What exploded with more force than before was a thick, black oily mess that you might associate with crude oil, black and evil and tendrilled with a meandering river of a mellow caramel-colored confluence that belied its malevolent nature. A violent, vicious, and viscous explosion that I almost was prepared for, but not quite. Again, it took about three different convulsions (what is it about threes anyhow) amounting to about another two quarts of the tar-looking stuff, and I thought that at least one of my internal organs was going along for the ride because I didn't know what else was in there trying to exit the program.

Plus, it involved pains akin to childbirth (only having witnessed a couple in person, vicariously) in reverse, if you can imagine such a thing.

Don't try. It only disturbs. I could go on but having something that tried to kill you in your head for a very long time and remembered with such painful reality kind of wears one out.

Well, after retching dry heaves for a while, I was afraid to move. The cramps and pounding in my head subsided somewhat, but I was still extremely nauseous, and my head was spinning, so I had to get to my bedroom on all fours. As I crawled into bed, I noticed through my window that the sun was going down, as was I, finally. So, after a very long day, uncaring that my sheets were soaked along with my mattress and pillow, it felt so good against my hot skin, that I fell asleep until the next morning, when I awoke very much in pain from head to toe.

Sore throat, unable to speak because my esophagus seemed to be made out of sandpaper. Barely able to swallow, I forced myself to squeeze down enough water to breathe. As I lay there, I was wondering how I had survived that, and vowed to never go through that again. I was not surprised at how all my muscles seemed torn because I could hardly move after the beating I just went through. Thanks to you, Al, for administering the kick-ass and to me for not paying attention and letting it happen. It's what my mom always told me, "Foolin' always turns into cryin'," and my mom was rarely wrong, when it came to this type of thing.

For the next couple of days, I nursed myself back to a type of normalcy. Starting with small sips of water, graduating to popsicles and anything cold and wet to soothe my tortured throat. After I hit the "chicken soup" stage, I knew I was going to be okay because the general nausea receded and my appetite started to return, but I remained muscle sore for another ten days. (It turned out later that I had ribcage muscle tears from the contortions I went through.) Just so you know, Dramamine does wonders for the nausea, at least afterward. As for the body aches, deal with it.

DELIBERATIONS UPON INTROSPECTION

I t turns out that I had lost 14 lbs. from start to finish that morning through the late afternoon—I guess a total of about eight hours because at the end of it the sun was going down, and it was early March when the sun sets a little early. To lose 14 lbs. of whatever it was after not having anything to eat or drink for the prior sixteen hours (I am including the hospital entrée the previous 6p.m. and the GI Joe a couple of hrs. before that) seems impossible. But I'm not a doctor, only a reporter in this little episode, and I have a few questions, if you don't mind. Since I was there, I'd just like to know what actually transpired inside the old GI tract. I know why because I am smart enough to realize how oblivious I was to the consequences of not paying attention. I am just wondering how it all works.

Considering that I had an empty stomach that morning and it took its sweet time filling me up from inside under tortuous conditions, not only once but three separate times, two quarts each, one more viscous and vicious than the last, is it some kind of osmosis? Since my hospital visit included a pretty good look at my private stuff, including my GI, I assume that if there was an issue, they would have probably extended my stay for another look. So I think I'm going to rule that out.

About ten days after my ordeal, I finally, feeling rather foolish, re-presented myself for re-inspection to my GP. When I explained the episode to my doctor, he commented that that little unsupervised adventure could easily have killed me. I didn't disagree. So I was a little surprised that he wasn't all that interested when I started to describe what had transpired. When his eyes started to glaze over as he looked at his watch, I figured that he's probably heard and seen it all before and another case of "anecdotal offal" was giving him "victim fatigue." Basically, he was sick and tired of hearing about it. Plus, he had other patients, and he was about to run out of them with me.

I imagine that since he's a doctor, he's been to a few demonstrations of alcohol addiction withdrawal in lectures, but I would be thrilled and amazed if he'd ever witnessed one of them in extremis. Like the hat trick three that I pulled off, a la cold turkey, without stepping in as referee. After all, experiments are meant to first seek experience and knowledge from results gleaned from multiple episodes of the same thing. The "do no harm" thing, when it comes to involving a human, would keep around the "curious to see what happens next crowd—like a train wreck, wanting to observe what is going on, but in good conscience, they would probably give up the train-wreck mentality and lend a hand or a hammer, depending on the circumstances, of course. So I am thinking that maybe the doctors' oaths to reinforce the general principle would have been adhered to. So again, I'm thinking no film.

Look, don't kill the messenger; I'm a mere traveling fool just like you. You dance to the melodies presented, unless you would rather hear something else. At that point sometimes improvisation is the best resolution, so go with that.

I understand that people who go into rehab programs voluntarily or otherwise are expecting to go through a minimal amount of discomfort, and that is most likely to be the case.

They do for the most part, I guess, because they or their enablers are able to get an appointment at the country club of their choice to get over the bad choices that they had already made in the first, second, or third places, and why not run for home. Safely ensconced and with no consequences, not even embarrassment, you come out fresh and new like the shiny copper penny that you somehow think will turn into gold by skipping the silver. You have to live through it in order to get over it, whatever it is. So stand up to reality and fix your own attitude and stop relying on everyone else to relieve your own internal pressure. Willpower is the power of your will, so depending on yourself is a good reason to understand that it's not too late to save someone's life, a valuable one, even if it's your own.

So they put you into a rehab place and hook you up to machines that will keep you alive and somewhat healthy while they keep you comfortable and semi-comatose so that you can recover and go merrily back to your version of social acceptance. Somehow you will miss the best and most important lesson to be learned, which is that in order to get over what it is that makes you want to escape from your reality will only be resolved by facing it. Even if it ends the life you are living right now.

And retrospection is the best memory to have because you have to ask yourself deep down if you really have anything to offer, and if you do, then bring it to the party, and we can all share in your concept. Rebuffed or accepted, at least you can be counted as a participant and not a mere observer, just by putting in your own two cent's worth. You can't sleep through such a thing, because you must decide what happened to your soul to arrive at the place you're in, the space you are in right now. Occupy a space that promotes resilience and truth. It is not enough for you to just skip the reading part and go to the cliff notes so that you recognize the tune. If it isn't your reality, you turn it off. Like sticking your thumbs in your ears and spare fingers over your eyes, barely looking with a squint through the Venetian blinds you manufactured to block the vision you see behind your frightened eyes. All the while saying "blah, blah, blah" to the universe. While deliberating with your angels, you might be able to understand just what in the hell did you think you were doing and why you are who you are and what just happened.

It won't become apparent if you are in a state where you are unable to access your own faculties and facilities, in the psychic sense as well as the physical. Sometimes it makes you wonder if the two are connected integrally and integrity wise, so that one will account to the other, as the symbiotic association is between the rest of your internal organs. If you are not in residence, then you are not there to open the door for your private soul to come in and advise you through either a spiritual breakthrough or a smackdown that will leave you almost dead.

Sleeping through the whole program does nothing but mitigate consequences to financial considerations. You can get through the pain and agony through a carefully induced coma that when it's over, it's a sigh of relief to have the episode erased from your reality. Remember the last time you went through a rehab program? Probably not, due to the fact that it was just a small respite, a vacation from your normal behavior, which is why you went there in the first place. And you can't wait to get back home where you can resume your personal party. A reverse bump.

After all, you'll likely be back when someone insists that they have had enough of you having too many conversations with Al or other cohorts more dangerous than you think and spewing venom on those closest to you. You don't think about that because you only veered off the tracks a little, but you can get back to normal just by being a "nice person." Until you are not anymore.

You check in to a rehab place not for a remedy but as an escape for a while from the ridicule that follows you around like the security blanket you proudly wear. For you are invincible, and the fact that your life may be already over doesn't take up a whit of your conscience. You think you have a new lease on life, except the foundation is already destroyed by something you can't buy with anything but introspection of your soul.

I keep going back to the soul thing because while traveling my highway to my B&B it was a constant battle with Al talking in one ear and my GA in the other, and it was like having a teleconference, wondering about this and that and transitioning that very painful long time into a meaningful conversation that led me to this point in my life. Which led me to writing this book. It seems that I would feel recalcitrant in my duties as a universal citizen if I didn't give you a heads-up when it comes to what your future destination could be when comeuppance time comes to visit, and you blink.

Pay attention to details. Even little ones. There are no regrets, as far as I am concerned, only memories of things I might have wished went the other way. And now you realize that the things you may have regretted are a god-send, and that good lessons are learned the hard way. Sleeping through the whole thing will teach you nothing except another way to escape reality. I can't blame you for taking the rehab escape route because the path I took should never be visited by anyone. It was too late for me because I wasn't expecting it. But considering your circumstances, suggesting more pain is not amenable to your situation. That is the reason for the heads up. Paying attention is key. Play with Al. He is a fun guy, but tolerant he is not, so tread lightly, because Al will try to kill you if you're having too much fun and will want to exit the party early without asking for permission to leave.

THE POINT ZERO SIX
PERCENT SOLUTION

I think enough said about previous circumstances, some controllable and some not, depending on your point of view. The present is here now and under your control.

I guess I'm writing this because maybe I'm not the only "baby boomer" (I'm sixty-five by way of 1954) whose life and Al's have crossed paths in the way described earlier. Care and fancy-free, you found a way to pleasantly stroll through your life by being a participant in normal society while also being a stand-up person who means no one any harm because you have the solution. The .06 one.

You know, you're kind of like the middle-class guy who comes home from work every night and has a conversation with Al in a "Hi, honey, I'm home" type situation where you don't expect an answer only the welcome you deserve for going to work every day or getting stressed from conversations you are having with your two ex-wives who happen to be the same woman and who might want to try for a third time, and I'm thinking that it's something about threes man it must be something about threes. ¥¥¥. Sorry, I guess I get a little sidetracked from time to time. So these daily conversations with Al get to be not quite an addiction but more of a habit. A prescription, if you will, that doesn't have to be a lengthy conversation or even deep, but a quick hello will suffice. After all, he does live with you, and you invited him to stay with you for as long as you need him, or it could be that he holds the cards and he will decide when to let you go. It's a "which came first" situation. But you are in charge, after all, aren't you? Because you keep your blood-alcohol level at .06 percent in certain and social situations so that you can walk and talk and drive at the same time. All perfectly legal and moral to keep you at the perfect altitude and attitude that suits your will. That's the power of your will. Use it before you lose it. Deciding *what* you do is *up* to you.

Yes, you are in charge. Since it's just you and me and Al, who's the fool now. If I am the scribe and Al is playing the tune, I'm wondering who is dancing, because there is always a tune playing somewhere. There is something about threes, each one of the parts necessary to sustain a triangle, and maybe that is the message in itself.

Being foolish is fun, but you have to know how to handle it. It depends upon the third side, the balancing act one. Kind of like the juggler in the old-time circus performances where amazing things were done with bowling pins and fire, sometimes simultaneously, and you wonder what it's like to live on the edge of danger. And so you do. Paying attention to your next step is crucial because the next might be your last.

You know, come to think of it, Al may be one of the only constants in your life, except the angst of the daily details you perform by rote. And the rituals you perform each day, such as taking the lifesaving meds you need for staying healthy, as the doctor has prescribed, don't seem enough to mellow your mood. Especially when you need a lightened or enlightened one.

So you wouldn't stop taking your lifesaving meds without your doctor's advice, and since you have been self-medicating for whatever reason for years, it may occur to you that you are the doctor and the patient, and you might just go through an accidental underdose.

You blinked. That brief interlude that takes your eyes off the road and produces something that you didn't quite expect. Like kissing an old oak that you think you might have avoided if you were paying attention. While it was at the top of your mind, you forget why you chanced the outcome but did it anyway. A very dangerous attitude for one who cares nothing about one's safety, regardless of consequences left in the aftermath. Being free and able are probably more important than personal safety to you, but responsibility is a necessary tool, so pay attention because it costs you nothing but self-respect.

There I go on another tangent, but is it really?

TO WIT

A s I alluded to earlier, Al is, was, and will always be around, one way or another. With all the money involved and with the captive audience enthralled, the industry has nowhere but up to go.

I wouldn't have it any other way. After all, capitalism is king as everyone knows.

Think of this scribe as a warning sign. Maybe it's Catholic guilt. As my sainted mother (God rest her soul) always said, "Always leave the world a little bit better off than when you arrived." A good plan. And rather than just bury this episode and chalk it up to experience and put it in a box on the shelf, I thought that sharing the truth of the story may be helpful. Maybe going through what I experienced—vicariously, at least—will help someone sidestep a life-threatening event.

It's all about paying attention, I think. I was just cruising along, good attitude, pleasant altitude, minor turbulence here and there, but no real hazards in sight. Daily conversations with Al weren't really an issue or necessary, I didn't think, because I was never out of touch with reality in my mind, but the mind somehow describes your circumstances, and maybe you took a wrong turn and ended up back from whence you came.

I understand that thirty-six to seventy-two hours of not touching base with Al will probably piss him off. That seems about right. My tipping point was around 40. As usual, I have a problem with middling, but meddling is not my deal, so you will do what your will wants and there lies the answer—did I say willpower?

Be that as it may, I would feel recalcitrant in my cosmic and civic duties if I failed to report that there may be danger ahead for those who have constant conversations with Al. When you get into a habit, you don't realize the slow deterioration of the things that keep you vital. Like if you chewed your fingernails growing up, and instead of going to a manicurist, when you get older, you are late to notice that unwittingly you have no fingers left, and who needs fingernails anyway?

It's something along those lines, except this one involves your soul. Just remember to advise Al that you're leaving if you do. And if you do, don't do it alone. He will be sorely pissed and may not forgive you. Also, invest in telling truth to health issues that are problematic because a doctor's good advice might save your life.

FRIENDS YET?

To those of you who are friends of Bill, please don't take umbrage at my attitude. I have been to a few meetings in my time, and while it's extremely important for those in attendance (it's obvious that some souls need more attention and comfort than others, and everyone sometimes needs a hand up) as a kind of group therapy, I found them a little depressing with the "How low can you go?" repertoire that is prevalent. Also, it's a shame to waste your angst on self-loathing exercises in one-downmanship loyalty (I can't get out of it, so why should you?) while the world is still afoot and awaiting. Take a step out of your comfort zone and contribute your expertise to the people around you. You may be useful after all.

Before all of your troubles, the ones that drove you to ask Al for advice and guidance and love every day, you probably started to ignore your friends because you never really had any anyway and Al was the best friend that you ever had. Always—sad but true. No matter, because getting back to the surface may keep you from drowning, and real friends will be there to hold your hand, if only for a while, until they're not. It may be a good idea to get out and about and enjoy life as you used to, unafraid of the sights and sounds that used to give you pleasure. It takes a while to get where you are, with careful determination, so don't be surprised that it takes a little longer to reintegrate into society. It's difficult to get addicted to Al because it comes from constant and consistent behavior, so it takes a while before your prescriptions kick in, and all of a sudden, you get the feeling that something is missing from your diet, so you come up with your solution (.06 percent), and it works for a while until you have to up your dosage so that your personal reality can stay within reach. That's when things start to go wacky, and you don't realize that by upping your script you're about to get ripped. Psychologically and personally, your foundations are gone, all being swept away with the broom of self-gratification. What, is that wrong? Your decision, your portal. Now what? Instead of a head on a shoulder looking for relief, why not a hand on one because help has arrived? And you know who is there, don't you? It might be you.

So if I can give any advice at all, it's actually a suggestion to help you get back to reality. The meetings are a good idea, because your confluence of consciousness at the time and place you're in at the same time means you can consider other options for fun, but in a different way. The same cognition, but a different fruition.

Say, for instance, you all get together in your regular group, but pick a local Irish pub for your meeting. If I know them, it's likely to be quite a mellow place during the day but quite the hopper at night. Get a table in the corner at the back so you can have the private conversations you usually do, and order some no-Al concoctions and watch the show. It can be quite amusing and nostalgic and gratifying to know that there, but for the grace of God, you go. Depending on your revulsion level, emotionally, of acquaintances of Al, it may be a good idea to pick your own poison, and only visit during low octane times, to break the ice of re-entry. It's okay to mingle with acquaintances, Al, you friends of Bill. You, of course, are the only measure of your courage. It may be time to reevaluate yourself regarding the asinine behavior you pulled off back in the day and got away with it, or so you thought at the time. It might be a kick or a kick in the ass, but maybe bravery knows no bounds. You'll never discover anything at all if you walk past all the open doors. As someone once said, "Can't we all just get along?"

To you acquaintances of Al, please pay attention to what lies down the road. As I've said many times, Al is not going anywhere, and despite the times he tied to kill me, accidentally or not, I'll decide when or if I'll talk to him next, not the reverse.

Two of my favorite sayings came from my dear departed mother (God rest your soul, Mom). The first is "Foolin' always turns into cryin'," followed by "Don't come cryin' to me when…" (you fill in the blanks depending on the situation).

Consider yourself warned by a fellow traveler.

There is a third one that was reserved for driving situations when all the unseatbelted kids were bouncing around being antsy (seatbelts? We don't need no stinking seatbelts!): "Don't make me come back there!" As if!

Top of the world, Ma!

W

CPSIA information can be obtained
at www.ICGtesting.com
Printed in the USA
LVHW040128080621
689672LV00005B/213